JOURNEY LEARNS TO PRAY

Daniel B Lancaster & Jeffrey Lancaster
Illustrated by Cindy Monroy & Sarah Hernández

FOR RHYS

Every night Journey and her mama snuggled in bed
As she listened to the bedtime stories she read.

When she finished, they held hands as she prayed
Thanking God for Journey and all she learned that day.

One night, Journey said, "I want to learn to pray, But I don't know how or what to say!"

To start we lift our hands in **PRAISE**
And give thanks for every new day.

We lift our hands to worship God
Because He's the one that made us all.

We praise God for the world He made
And for His peace when we feel afraid.

We thank Him for our family and friends
And for His blessings that never end.

Then, we make things **RIGHT** with God
And tell Him the times that we've done wrong.

We shape our hands into a heart
Because God gives us a brand-new start.

Just like how I wash your messy clothes

God makes your heart as white as snow.

ASKing God for help is the next part of prayer.
We know He loves us and really cares.

We hold out both hands to receive
Because it honors God when we believe.

And comfort hurting boys and girls.

We end our prayer by saying YES
To whatever God says 'cause He knows best.

Hold up your hands like you're honoring a king
'cause God is the ruler over everything.

Here's an easy way to remember each step
They spell PRAY - that's hard to forget!

 Is for **PRAISE** ...
Thank God for what He's done.

 Is for **RIGHT** ...
Tell God what you've done wrong.

 Is for **ASK** ...
Ask God for what we need.

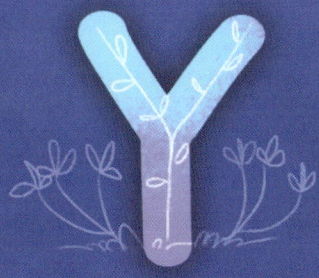 Is for **YES** ...
We follow God wherever He leads.

Just like when you learned to ride your bike
Your prayers will get better the more you try.

You can always ask me if you need help
But soon you'll find what works best for yourself!

THANKS FOR READING MY BOOK!

IF YOU ENJOYED IT PLEASE LEAVE A REVIEW ON AMAZON SO MORE KIDS CAN FIND IT AND LEARN HOW TO PRAY.

go.lightkeeperbooks.com/journeyprays

JOIN MY LIGHTKEEPER KIDS CLUB TO RECIEVE A PDF WITH COLORING PAGES AND MORE TIPS ON HOW TO PRAY!

ASK AN ADULT TO SIGN YOU UP AT:

go.lightkeeperbooks.com/kidsclub

Text copyright © 2020 by Daniel B Lancaster
Cover art and interior illustrations copyright © 2020 by Cindy Monroy and Sarah Hernández
All rights reserved.
ISBN 979-8736497706
Lightkeeper Books

"Very sweet! Easy for kids to understand and relate to!"

Visit **go.lightkeeperbooks.com/lkk** to learn more

MORE FROM THIS AUTHOR

#1 Best Sellers

on

This series on powerful prayer, heart-felt worship, and intimacy with Christ will help strengthen your "War Room" and give you a battle plan for prayer.

Visit go.lightkeeperbooks.com/battleplan to learn more.

CHRISTIAN SELF-HELP

NEW Series!

Available on amazon

Overcome fear, shame, and other spiritual attacks that hold you back from being all God created you to be.

Visit go.lightkeeperbooks.com/selfhelp to learn more.

Coming SOON

DEATH IS A LIAR

Find hope and healing in your grief journey. *Death Is A Liar* offers practical, compassionate help for those suffering in the valley of the shadow of death.

Printed in Great Britain
by Amazon